DIALOGUES FROM MY DWAM

PRERNA

Made with ♥ on the Notion Press Platform
www.notionpress.com

"TO THE LOVE THAT IS UNBOUND...."

Contents

Preface

Behind a chirpy facade, there lay a quiet overthinker. Often lost in my dwam, my reveries, my mind wandered not just to my experiences but it traveled far and wide to conceived notions, probabilities, what ifs, and what nots. I had actual conversations with myself and poems were born.

This collection of poetry should find a place in every heart that has ever loved. Most of it comes from a place of empathy and a keen perspicacity for those who have enjoyed and endured the offerings of love.

Happy Reading!

Acknowledgements

"Silent gratitude isn't much use to anyone"-Gertrude Stein

Let me shout out a loud thank you to the man whose nudges have always been the most effective. 'Go on, write some more,' he would say this more often than I could count. And to the one who would send me in my reverie. This book is because he is. To A&P.

Chapter 1

My clock struck twelve,
a little too early
I had to head back home,
An arduous journey
for it wasn't where my heart was.
My escapades in the arms of solitude
cut short.
Duty called,
Laden with reality, I returned.
Soaked in dreams
I walked along the glorious corridors
of chimeric fantasies.
Only to be rudely awakened
into the mundaneness.
Worldliness beckoned,
The heart yearned
for its fairyland retreat
But the clock had struck
And the mirage was waning.

Chapter2

I find you in me,
quietly occupying a place.
Yet your presence
resonates loud.
Unknown to me
for years,
the essence of my being now.
A thread invisible yet enduring,
ties me to you.
Unbothered by the distance,
unaffected by the absence.
My shameless adulation,
resolute and determined
like a solemn oath.
A desire,
Contained but aching to pour out.
To find me in you,
Just the way you live in me.

Chapter3

The warmth of your embrace
steeps in my bones.
I bathe in your love,
soaking like a sponge.
A fleeting touch
sending shivers to my soul.
As every tiny bit of you
takes up the biggest space in me.
The sky isn't the limit
for devotion is infinite.
Body and beyond
my submission to you.
And all I seek
is a gentle promise.

Chapter 4

My cheeks hurt,
I am smiling a little too hard.
The dimples are singed ,
holding those salty drops for too long .
I come back empty handed ,
conned and ripped off.
Forever cosseted those I held close,
now I have thrown away the concern.
Pollyannaish till the end,
I have ceased the merry chase.
Unsparing in my offerings,
squeezed out to the final drop.
Spent and hollowed out,
I am an exhausted mine.
Abandoned for heaping carcasses ,
raptors screeching in my ears.
My moribund state giving away
to the ultimate call .
There is a seeming gaiety
but my cheeks still hurt.

Chapter5

I am looking for a mirror
to your mind
To gaze at the reflection to
feel its depth
To read your muted musings
and unvoiced thoughts
To decipher your boundaries
and your scope

*

I am looking for a window
to your soul
To peek in and maybe understand
your silences
To listen to every word that you
never uttered but felt
To seek answers to my doubts
and settle in the finality

Chapter6

The flowers are blooming
The fragrance has waned
The colours are vivid
Yet the sheen is lost
The wind blows through my hair
The whiff smells stale
My sun shines sharp
But often eclipsed
The choir sings songs
The tune melancholy
Dancers in rhythm
To timbres dull
And I sit and wonder
What is wrong with my paradise

Chapter 7

Voyaged halfway,
that's when I found you.
Both done and dusted,
yet seeking a station.
Spirited still,
sedulously I built
a castle, airy yet grounded.
Securing happiness
even if for a little while.
For love begets love,
so I shall be blessed.
And though I know
my boat's been rocking
I can see the shore in sight.
The beacon's glowing.
I have come this far
Trusting the magic
of new beginnings
on the midway.
It's time to set the anchor,
For I have found land in you.

Chapter8

Some connections
Unseived yet unadulterated
Some Emotions
honest yet discreet
Some feelings
Powerful yet gentle
Some ties
Firm yet yielding
Some bonds
Obvious yet complex
Some relations
Close yet buried

Chapter 9

It creeps in, stealthily
Sneaks from behind
and engulfs me
Picking me in crowds
where I attempt to camouflage
I flee, in vain
Ubiquitously, it descends on me
I seek escape
in feigned laughter
Yet I find myself
drenched in its colour
A tinge leaking
through the corner of an eye
Loneliness takes over
yet again.

Chapter10

Your avowal is awaited,
Like the closing flourish
to my endeavours.
A brush of sheen,
the final coat on a painting.
Like the last piece of a jigsaw puzzle,
giving meaning to the incoherent mess.
The dragging play of emotions
needs a curtain fall on the show.

Chapter 11

There is an order amidst chaos
A calm within the tempest
Silence concealed behind the violence
And peace on the heels of mayhem

There is a knowledge within unlearning
Wisdom in the realms of ignorance
Darkness beneath the flame's glow
And enlightenment awaiting in unlit caves

Care resides in words of admonition
Concern tucked under caution
Progress often lies in severance
And love blossoms when you let go

Chapter12

I wish to learn
the story of your scars,
From the blow that struck
and the blood that flowed.
As you winced in pain,
did you let out a scream?
Or did your strong face prevail,
like it always does?
I imagine comforting you,
Your head on my bosom.
Cleansing your wound,
with the flow of my love.
When the blood dried up,
and the scab hardened,
did you pick on the pain
lest you forget the cause?
Did you seethe,
and kindle the fire?
Or have you chosen peace
as you outline the mark?
Do you feel marred?
Do they reveal your pride?

PRERNA

I yearn to hear
when your scars tell.

Chapter 13

Entangled wires
Withering flowers
Paling papers
Dimming lights
These are stories of the yore
Crescendoing laughter
Flourishing fields
Blooming buds
Full moon nights
My lyrics, getting a makeover
The cerulean seas
Golden sands
The infinite skies
And empyrean spaces
Tapestries to weave my words

A Mother's affection
Lovers' union
Doting devotees
An artist's expression
The essence of my verses

Chapter14

It wasn't easy
To unlearn convenience
And to dare the different
For it wasn't meant to be ordinary
It wasn't easy
Crossing undefined boundaries,
Entering obscure lands
Armed with the certitude of acceptance.
It wasn't easy
To be magical enough
Yet looking for pixie dust in your words
To give me a flight
It wasn't easy
Giving you my most fragile part
Knowing well that you could break it easily
But knowing well again,
that you wouldn't.

Chapter15

My convoluted thoughts tangled,
A mystery waiting to be unravelled.
Complications of myriad emotions
in the hydraheads of my feelings,
emerging only to be crushed once again.
Journeying on a forked street,
Tough choices, tougher decisions
None completely winning.
But a path I must take
To relinquish pride and choose love
Or to give up on the heart
and settle upon maturity?

Chapter16

My limits are my strengths
Holding on to them
I endure
An acceptance of my flaws
An agreement with my follies
I advance
My foibles make me fall often
Yet I am unstoppable
Focused, absorbed
The daunting task ahead
Formidable, dispiriting
Yet I do not falter
For I know, I am wanting
In identity
My name, a mere pile of letters
Desire a meaning
No, the flesh isn't weak
And the spirit is willing
Take note, celebrate, acknowledge
For I am
On the road to Elysium
I am arriving.

Chapter 17

The maniacal noises
of worldliness
invading my peace.
The squabbling sounds
of humanity
disturbing my calm.
A tempest building
under the stoic silence
of the surface.
Forbearing to the eyes,
a rebellion grows underneath.
The heart covets your heart,
to quell the mutinous thoughts.
Come and silence the storm
with your sorcery.
Heal the wound
and I shall sleep again .

Chapter18

Places unknown beckon me,
as I wander into nothingness.
Seeking a bit of the nihility,
I venture through oblivion.
Deriving comfort from the escape,
finding solace in solitude.
The crowd I had left behind jeered,
teasing me with taunts of failure.
I continued walking sedated,
derision making me more determined.
As I walked towards limbo,
I discover my light in the darkness.

Chapter19

How do I unlove you,
Unfeel the feelings?
How do I do the undoable?
Like flaming the sun
An effort, in vain.
Like erasing the creases on the palms.
A try, to no end.
It hurts,
to be failed,
repeatedly, repetitively.
You hear the words I say,
Failing to listen to the ones I don't.
And yet I choose ignominy,
as I continue loving you,
unabated and persistent.
Rooting for you
as I keep losing ground.
The broken parts of me,
define me.
While my dying breaths
try to keep the flame alive.
It is my last hurrah.

Chapter20

I painted a dream,
on a canvas I had woven.
I picked bright colours,
but they turned out pale.
A stirring theme,
yet a vapid outcome
The tools were replaced,
the palette switched.
I twisted a few patterns,
the confusion persisted .
The fervour never waned,
my passion boosted.
Failures failing to
take me down.
Hours consumed,
days devoured.
Aching fingers,
numbing mind.
My masterpiece
never came to life.
The canvas lay covered
in streaks and smears.

Chaotic lines and
incoherent patterns.
I stood dejected
crestfallen and looted.
The brushes lay strewn,
the colours ruined.
Stains on my face,
smudges on my being.
Perhaps it was time
to burn the canvas.